I COUNT MY BLESSINGS

Amy Moone

Dedicated to the woman
Who showed me how a mother
Loves unconditionally.
Who listened and gave me advice.
Who lifted me up and supported me.
Who comforted me on my dark days.
I love you, and am truly blessed
To have met you and have you in my life.

♡ your sister

Amy
Moore

AUTHOR'S NOTE

Please be aware as you read that not all of these poems are based on true events. Some such as the ones involving suicide or the death of a loved one, are poems that came to me and I feel reflected my thoughts and feelings of the time. Others, such as The Dream and Them, are based on real dreams or experiences I had. These poems are spanning my life from middle school up to my 30's. I put them together as a therapeutic exercise to work through my experiences and feeling. If even one of the following poems touches your heart and resonates with your feelings, then I have achieved my goal.

PART ONE

MY LIFE BEFORE

Them

They live upstairs,
They pay the bills.
One goes to work,
Day after day.
While the other
Stays at home.

They watch TV,
While I try to talk.
They say "we hear you"
But don't actually listen.
They form opinions
From info they've heard.
Most coming from me,
When in the heat of arguments.

They say they love me,
But they don't show it.
They call me names.
They put me down.
They make me feel uncertain,
And sometimes I hate them.

They are my mom
And my step dad.
They make promises
Then they forget.

They make me wish
For a different life.

They chase me,
Make me hate some reality.
They say I spend too much time alone,
When what I'm doing is trying to escape.
They make me mad and sad.
They make me cry.
They seem to enjoy it.
They tease and poke.

They make me turn to books
And my other hobbies
To get away from the hurt and the pain
That they give to me.
They never cease
To push me at least once a week.

They talk about me
When they think I don't hear.
But I always pause and listen
For what I know they say.
They never disappoint me there,
They always have a mean thing to say.

They live upstairs.
They pay the bills.
They push me hard.
So I now know my future plans.
I plan to go away,
To leave the ones who live upstairs.
They are my mom and my step dad.

You Think I Don't Care

You think I don't care
That I don't see it.
I see more than you think.

Do you notice?
I'm starting to think that
You don't notice as much
As I used to think.
I'm starting to think that
you only see what
you really want to.

You accuse me of not
Seeing or asking.
But I do.
Does that mean you just
Want to make me feel bad?

Well if it does,
It worked.
Or maybe it's not me
That I feel bad about,
But rather you and
What you think.

Girl in the Mirror

Who's that girl I see in the mirror?
The one with the long brown hair.
The one with the deep blue eyes.
The one who wears my red lips.

Who's that girl I see in the mirror?
The one with the troubled eyes.
The one with eyes filled with frustration, pain and
hatred.
The one whose eyes match mine, but with more emotion.

Who's that girl I see in the mirror?
The one with thin red lips.
The one with those lips looking haunted, troubled.
The one whose lips curve opposite my own

Who's that girl I see in the mirror?
The one with my clothes on.
The one with my body and hair.
The one who looks just like me, but also doesn't.

Who's that girl I see in the mirror?
She's the one who hides inside, never to be seen.
She's the one who hides my emotions so others don't see
them.
She's the one that takes the pain and hurt and bears it so
I don't have to.

She's my best and truest friend.
She's my inner self.

Smiles

Smiles,
They hide a lot.
They hide anger,
Love, sadness, and not.
They show
Only what we let them.
They are like dresses,
Without the hem.
They are clothing
Over our true feelings.
Without them
We have no bearings.

The Dream

I dream that I'm with my uncle in a car,
Driving somewhere with trees.
I dream that we stop somewhere,
In among the trees.
I dream that he tries to grab me,
Of me saying "no" pleadingly.
I dream that we're back at grandma's,
Of all my relatives being there.
I dream that all of the sudden all I'm wearing is a coat,
Of him trying to take it off, deaf to my pleas.
I dream of desperately pleading "no",
Of him so cruelly persisting.
I dream of breaking away
Of running crying to the kitchen.
I dream of desperately crying to my mom,
Of her saying she didn't see.
I dream I run back to the living room,
Of looking for a place to go.
I dream of running into a hidden room,
Of feeling him smiling behind me.
I dream of waking my aunt,
Of her saying sorry and leaving.
I dream of looking for some clothes,
Of seeing only others' clothes.
I dream that I finally find some,
Of putting them on.
I dream of sitting on a couch,

Of crying and soon my cousin comes in.
I dream of us telling each other
What we like about each other.
I dream that two of my other cousins come
Of them asking me to go outside with them.
I dream that I say "no", of being afraid of him,
Of them saying that they'd protect me.
I dream of us walking outside,
Of bravely walking past him.
I dream of him thinking it was amusing
That I was trying to protect myself.
I dream of walking up a hill with my cousins
Of seeing a lot of people camped in the driveway.
I dream of them telling me to sit and wait for them
Of them giving me something sweet to drink.
I dream of seeing ruins
Of getting impatient and ascending the ruin stairs.
I dream of another uncle and grandma
Of them climbing with me, comforting me.

For days after this dream I remain afraid
Of what it might mean.
I remain afraid still, months later,
Of what might still happen.
So as I write this,
My recounting of my most frighteningly real dream,
I let go of some of that fear.

Outsider

Ever feel like you don't belong?
Like you're an outsider?
Well, I'll describe it for you.

It's when you're with your friends
But you're withdrawn into yourself.
It's when you have all kinds of stuff
You want to say but can't.
When you just don't want to talk
Even to your best friend.
It's like depression,
But you're not depressed at all.
It's when you think you know someone
Then find out you don't.
It's always being the sensitive
Or fall back person.
When your friends are happy
But even if you're not you pretend.

Ever feel like you don't belong?
Like you're an outsider?
Well if you have and even if you haven't,
Watch others to see if they do.
Because I know how they feel.

I Saw It All

I saw him walk in the room
He scanned the bar as if looking for someone
I saw his eyes stop at you and wished it was me
You two were like magnets, instantly attracted to each
other
I saw how good you looked together
And wished it were me instead of you

I saw your first, second and third dates
Along with all of the following ones
I saw the first time he kissed you
The first time he held you in his arms
I saw you fall in love
I had long since fallen

I saw him sneak around on you
I was the other woman
I saw the look of hurt in your eyes
The night you caught us together
I saw him run to you

To try and comfort you, telling you you were the one he
really loved

I saw you almost cave to him
Before steeling yourself and walking out
I saw him crumple to the floor

Confused at how he got to this point
I saw you crying the next day
But didn't dare approach you

I saw the marks on your arms in the following weeks
The ones you tried to hide
I saw past the long sleeved shirts
Past the bracelets on your arms
I saw into your heart
Because I had been there too

I saw you on the path to self-destruction
And he was so upset and confused, he was no help
I saw him keep trying to talk to you
But you kept pushing him away
I saw you look at me forlornly many times
I was too ashamed to look you in the eye

I saw that you were missing one day
Everyone was asking about you
I saw your mother in the store
And she told me what you'd done
I saw her grief and almost hugged her
But she gave me a look that said she knew it was my
fault

I saw all this happen but was unable to stop it
Or maybe unwilling is the better word
I saw how much you two had loved each other

As your best friend I should have been happy for you
I saw your hurt after you found out about us
I should have tried to talk to you, to explain

I saw your life unfold
Like I was watching a movie
I saw all of us get tangled up
In a web of lies and deceit and betrayal

I saw the ending of the story when the story began
But I did nothing to stop it

Goodbye My Love

You poke and stir the ash, flesh, and bone.
That's all that's left but a few charred memories.

Your class ring that you gave to me
The day you asked me to go steady.
The necklace you gave to me
For our first Valentine's Day.
The diamond pendant you gave to me
The day you first told me of your love.
The simple gold ring that you gave to me
To represent your future promises to me.

The memories in my mind are so clear still.
The memory of the love in your eyes,
The comfort I felt from your eyes that held me tight.
The love and joy I felt
When you said, "it's forever."
The joy in your eyes
When I said, "yes."

The look you had on your face
The day you told me you were sorry.
That it didn't mean anything, not really.
It was a one-time mistake,
Never would you let it happen again.

The emotions I felt when I heard what you had done.
The sorrow and deep sense of betrayal.
How could you?
You, the only one who loved me back?
Why would you ever make a mistake like that?
Didn't you know how it'd hurt me?

When the fire broke out in my room
From a fallen candle I had lit,
I just laid there and waited
Not caring if it was over.
I didn't want to live,
Not anymore.
I can't stand the pain
I'll go quietly.

Goodbye, my love.
I wish you luck.
I hope the baby's healthy
And that you can be happy.

From somewhere above
I watch you.
You're crying over my ashes,
Apologizing for all you did.

I wish you could hear me now.
Because I'd tell you
That I still love you
And even though I don't understand,
I forgive you and wish you the best.
Goodbye, my love.

They

They are disgusting.
How can you stand them?
Are they in your class?
They're retarded.
They're weird.
They're not like us.
They have no home.
Don't hang around them.
They're crazy.
They're suicidal.
They're depressed.
They aren't normal.
They do drugs.
They drink.
They hate everyone.
They aren't one of us.

They are perfect.
They think we're inhuman.
They see what they want,
and nothing more.
They get good grades.
They are cheerleaders
and jocks.
They drive nice cars.
They're considered normal.
They call us weird.

To us they're weird
and we're normal.
They don't understand.
They don't even try.
They ignore us,
and give us looks.

Who's "they"?
Is it the ones who are
considered normal?
Or the ones considered weird?
To the "normal" ones,
"they" are the "weird" ones.
To the "weird" ones,
"they" are the "normal" ones.
To the ones in the middle,
"they" is both groups.

Hurt

I hurt you,
I didn't mean to,
But you hurt me too.

I hurt my friend.
She only tried to help,
But she didn't know,
What it's like being hurt.

I hurt my family.
They didn't know what was wrong,
But they knew when I hurt them.

I hurt everyone I loved.
Who's left to hurt but me.

I hurt myself,
There was no one else.
They all hate me now.
I hurt myself,
And now no one else can.

Customer Service

Another day in customer service
Another money transfer
A customer wants a refund
Says the person they sent to
Didn't get the money
Okay, Okay
Call the company
Wait on hold for twenty minutes
Listening to the same ads over and over
Finally get a person
Give them the store info
Tell them the reference number
Wait for them to pull up the file
They say the money has been received
Thank them and hang up
Explain to the customer
"So I can't get a refund?"
Count to ten in head
Politely explain again
No, the person already got the money
"So I can't get the money back?"
Breathe and count to ten
AGAIN tell them no, they cannot have a refund
They frown and leave
You sigh and go to the next person
Just another day in customer service.

PART TWO

MY DREAMS AND ESCAPES

Suffocating

I can't breathe
Something is over my head.
It's slowly cutting off my air.
It stinks of acid.
I can see a person
Through the foggy bag.
They laugh at me,
They did this to me.
The ones who pretend
To be my friends.
The ones who lied to me
To make me turn away
From those true.
They made me think
That the world is full
Of people like them.
They are the ones
Who do this to me now.
I can feel my body
Panicking with every labored breath.
I know I'm dying.
They do too and they're glad.
What did I do
To make them mad?
What did I do
To make them want to kill me?

Suddenly,
As I take my last breath,
I wake up and find I'm still in bed.
I was dreaming
That I was suffocating.
What does it mean?

What The Moon Saw

She whimpers
Nudging her mother
Stillness
She licks the red wound
Blooming on her mothers chest
Silence
She paws her mother's nose
Watching for any movement
Whining
Her ears pinned to her head
Tail pulled in tight
Crickets
Night noises restart
The danger has passed
Dead
Her mother was dead
Never to move again
Sadness
She raises her eyes
Seeing the moon above
Sing
She sings of her mother's passing
Sings of her loneliness
Silence
As the moon watches over her
Howls begin to answer her
Rustle

A wolf steps from the brush
Another follows
Pack
The alpha female nudges the pups mother
She lifts her head and sings
Howl
The rest of the pack joins her
Voices joined in sorrow
Sorrow
One by one the wolves head to their den

The alpha female picks up the motherless pup
Witness
The moon saw it all
The hunter, the wolf and pup, the pack

Internal Struggles

I am sitting at the window staring out on Mother Nature.

I am thinking about life and its meaning.

I am wondering why people act the way they do.

I am listening for to the sweet harmony of the wolves singing in my mind mingled with the real sounds outside.

I am struggling to figure out how I feel about life, people, about myself and my actions.

I am silently crying with the tears forming small streams down my cheeks.

I am trying to figure out the reason behind these tears.

I am startled to feel a comforting hand on my shoulder and fingers gently running through my hair and down my back.

I am waiting to see if he will say anything.

I am hoping that he won't go away, that he'll take me in his arms and hold me.

I am disappointed when I turn to see him and no one's there.

I am saddened to realize that he was just a dream; he wasn't there at all.

I am back to looking out the window and listening to the wolves' forlorn
  cries in my head.

I am back to my internal struggle.

The Night You Died

That night so long ago that I most remember,
We were both so happy.
We were going to the movies.
It was our 6th anniversary.
You were 26, I was 24.
We were talking , and you leaned over to kiss me.
Neither of us saw the truck coming straight at us.
It hit us while we were still kissing, hit us straight on.
Some glass hit you in the side of the neck,
Your blood was everywhere.
Something hit my head,
I later found out it was the trucker's beer bottle.
I got knocked out.

When I woke up, they told me you were dead.
At first I didn't believe them.
Its our 6th anniversary I told them,
And we're going to the movies.
They told me we were on our way
When that drunk driver's truck
Came into our lane and hit us.
I never got to say goodbye,
Who'd have thought
That something so terrible could happen to us.
But it did, and has to many other like us.
I'll always that night, 60 years ago.
The night you died.

Distractions

I look out the window and see butterflies.
I start singing to the radio.
I see my friends' mouths move,
Them looking at me.
I know I should be listening,
Really I do.
But I just can't focus enough.

I look back out the window.
I imagine seeing a white wolf
Watching me in the moonlight.
I hear my name,
I look back at my friends
And say "Huh? What'd you say?"

Really its not my fault.
I just can't concentrate.
Its like my eyes and mind work
But not my ears.
Try as I might
I can't understand them.

My gaze wanders once again
But this time the vision I see is wondrous.
A huge pair of shimmering eyes
Looks at me in amusement.
I follow the eyes to see a golden dragon.

My friends give up and leave me in my dreamland.
More fantastic distractions follow the dragon.

Fairies, unicorns, pegasi, even unisi (unicorns with
wings).
I love my beautiful distractions.

Fire Maiden

She perches in a tree,
Where she longs to be.
Her robe of fire settled around her,
Like a fire consuming her.

Yet it's not yet her time to go,
And when it is everyone will know.
She will open her mouth and scream,
As the fire washes over her like a stream.

This time it will bring tears to her eyes,
Because this time she won't re-rise.
All her kind are gone,
There's no reason for her to live on.

Then the time is near,
She doesn't fear,
Around the world people feel her scream,
Her silent tears form a stream.

Her precious feathers become ash,
And fall to the ground in a gray flash.
The ash falling like a quiet rain,
She's gone, never to rise again.

If I had Wings

I spread my coal black wings
And raise my face to the sun
The warmth washing over me
A breeze stirs my feathers
Keeping them cool
Water droplets settle on my skin
Like dew in the early morning
I look over the edge of the cliff below me
Watching the water fall hundreds of feet
To crash into the lake below
I smile and take a step forward
Diving down
My wings closed
My hair whipping behind me
I watch the my reflection in the waters surface
Get closer and closer
Finally a few feet from hitting
I flip open my wings
I reach down and skim my fingers over the water
Laughing with delight
I see the deep part of the lake in front of me
Slowing I pull my wings in and dive into the cool water
I swim to the bottom before turning and
Pushing my body back up shooting out of the water
Back in the sky droplets rain from my skin
My feathers dry quickly as I flap them to gain height
I hover and survey the land

Knowing I can go anywhere
My wings can take me

I sigh as my alarm blares
I open my eyes and sit up in my bed
Looking behind me
Still feeling the weight of wings
Sad to see them gone
The dream leaves me missing a freedom I'd only know
If I had wings

Mistaken

He had told her over and over
How much he loved her
How much he needed her
How he'd never leave her
She had given in to his wishes
But when she told him 3 months later
He left her alone
Saying she was mistaken
Saying he didn't want this
Saying she was trying to trap him

The next few months she was sullen
She was even more prone to tears
She was forced to eat by friends
She was fussed over by her mother
Everyone was worried about her

They saw her falling deeper and deeper into herself
Then one day she felt movement
It shifted inside her growing belly
It felt alive and a part of her
It seemed to be saying it needed her

She began to change after that
She would smile and touch her stomach
She took much better care of herself
She got that happy glow of a mother-to-be

She was happier than even before he left
She took charge of her life again
When she got her first ultrasound picture
She proudly showed everyone
She said she would raise her son
She would teach him to be a great man

She was not mistaken.

Dreaming

Dreaming
then waking.
Wanting to
but can't.
Freedom to do it all
that's all I want.

Dreaming
is freedom.
India is the place
you are the person.

Awake
time to face reality.
It's not real.
Reality comes busting in.
Rudely awakening me
jolting me from you.

It was wonderful
I want to go back.
I want to dream
forever.

Recurring Dream

I sit by a lake
On a low mountain top
Not high enough to be real cold.
Birds are chirping
Squirrels argue with the chipmunks
Deer cautiously drink from the lake

Night slowly falls
Birds quiet down
I begin to hear
Wolves
Calling to each other
I smile and wait
The wolves creep forward
They gather near me

I lay down
Submissive
Showing my belly
And my trust
The alpha male nudges the female
She licks me
Letting me know I can sit up
I slowly shift to the soft grass
And lay there among the pack.

PART THREE

MY BLESSINGS

Awakening

Nervousness
its been a long time
a long dusty drive
arriving at our destination
my breath being taken away
immediately the sense
of peace and love enfold me in their arms
I have to go see the willow

I touch its leaves and feel its life
I know its been there a long time and seems ageless
I wonder how many it has watched over
how many loves were born under those branches
how many kids wept their sorrows
and lived their joys under its watchful gaze
I can almost feel the magic
it threatens to carry me away and I am not afraid
it feels right
it feels safe

we talk and I watch the water while I hold onto the
willow's drapes
it supports me and holds me up
keeping me grounded
I feel I could float away
as we talk we hit sore subjects
subjects that hurt us both

but the peace and love surrounds me
and I feel myself letting all the bad things go
no caution, doubts, or negative feelings remain
they are very gently blown by the tiny breeze that stirs
around us

we talk a long time
eventually we go back to the little beach
so you can swim
I stand there, restless but peaceful
I take a picture of the beauty around me
knowing every time I look at it I'll feel the same peace
and love

we leave and go back to the house
the peace follows
I can let go and be me and I know this
I feel so free and open
we go to your room and talk
much of it serious and deep
we both trust the other with the stuff we won't tell others
I know we are passing a border but it feels right
so I let it go on not wanting to stop feeling so good

we eat dinner and talk to your mom
it feels so comfortable
you take my hand
I know that's past that invisible line
but it feels right
you accept me for who I am

we take a walk
to keep you awake

we go to a cemetery
which should feel weird but I like them
I tell you my theory about trees being guardians
you don't laugh at me
I look away from you towards the cemetery
and feel a pull from a tree
I've never felt that before
I tell you I need to go meet the tree
not really thinking of what I am saying
you just smile and say ok

I feel ready to burst into song
the joy I feel here among the trees
with you
we reach the tree and I almost hug it
I settle for running my fingers over its bark
looking at its many branches
we talk about how long they must have been there
how much they must have seen
I feel so full of love and peace that I could burst
as I look around other trees call to me
I tell you I want to meet the others
I look to you with a little doubt
wondering if you'll judge my actions
you smile a wonderful smile and tell me you love seeing
me like this
seeing how I glow

I smile, I can feel the glow you are talking about
I feel wonderful
we wander around the whole cemetery
I think I meet almost every tree
you even bring my attention to a few I almost overlook

we talk to my twin a little
she's half asleep and doesn't understand whats going on
I continue to linger at the trees
some I give into my urge to hug them
the sun starts going down
you point out the beautiful sky
I know we need to head back so I can begin my drive
home
I feel sad having to leave

but you and I talk about going back
and I know I'll feel that way again
I can't help but wonder
why those feelings were awakened that day
but I know it was meant to be
I will never regret it
just as I will never regret anything that happened
that day or the days following
I feel more like myself
like I know more of myself
and you gave me that confidence
I know this for sure

I know that day touched you too
but for me it was more than just your company
the environment
my renewed faith
and you, most definitely you were a big part
opened my eyes and my heart
I still feel that peace surrounding me
even among the hustle and bustle of work
but it is strongest when I talk to you
when I remember that day

you are and always will be close to my heart
whether as a dear friend
 a brother
roommate
or whatever life may bring
you helped me feel more comfortable in my own skin
and that means a lot to me
you've told me how much I've helped you
this is one way I can tell you how you've helped me

Moonlit Walk

Walking along the beach
Waves washing over my toes
Then gently
    Pulling
        Away
My breath echoes the gentle pull
In
    Out
In
    Out
My body relaxes as
Stress
    Flows
        Away
Caught on the waves
Work
School
Relationships
All the bad stuff
Gets
    Pulled
        Away
I sigh in content
Waves continue to wash over my feet
I smile
    Happy

The moon
     Shines
          Beautifully
Reflecting off the water
He appears ahead of me
Excitement
     Love
          Running
               Hugging tightly
We stand there
     Together
          Watching
The moon on the water
Relaxing
     Content
          To just be
               Together.

Anxiety

A tight panic squeezing my heart
Breaths coming fast and hot
My stomach twisting
The furious need to fidget
Or pace the floor
My brain scrambling
To find escape routes

A mass of people pressing in
Suffocating me
Invading my space
My muscles freeze up
Trying desperately
Not to cry

Just a thought of
Being around people
Of snaking through crowds
Of interacting
Of being judged
Makes me feel
Like an animal being hunted

Even being at a family gathering
Or a group of friends
Can cause the panic
The feeling of judgment

The awkwardness
Of not knowing what to say
Or do
What if it's wrong?

Leaving the house
Becomes a hurdle
To overcome
To get past
Wanting to be alone
To not have to fight
The fear, the panic
The nausea, my own brain
Books, music, movies
Become an escape
Cuddling a pet
Offers some comfort

Even on-line interactions
Are sometimes
Impossible
Even family
Can be too much
On those days
I withdraw into myself
I read or watch movies
I escape into worlds
Where I am brave
Fearless
Not broken

Daily Grind

A crash of sound
Hits me like a wave
Voices raised
Music playing
Machines running
My audio book
Trying to drown
Out the noise

I cringe and
Try to distract myself
Focus on my work
Or my solitaire game
The wave swells
I wince
All I want is quiet

Calm
Silence
Sounds I choose
Release
From the suffocation
Of the noise that
Continues to crash
Over me

I try to block them
Turn my mind
To daydreams
And thoughts
To stories
Who distract

My phone rings
I glance at it
And frown
My irritation grows
Why
Is quiet so hard
To come by

The lift screeches
Grating painfully
Tearing at my ears
I dig out ear plugs
The noise is dulled
My ears feel full
And strange
The noise still
Irritates
But is dulled
For the moment

I breathe a sigh
Of relief
When quitting time comes
All that remains is
To drive home
To get through traffic

To skip the store
For another night
I have enough to get by

I escape home
Where I can choose
Quiet and
The sounds I like
Where my world
Can calm
And people fade
Away

Digital World

Once I escaped by leaving the house
When that didn't work
I escaped into the world of books
That worked to a degree
But still the feeling was there
Then I discovered the digital world
With many places to explore
But still I felt the need
Felt it build and build
Then I discovered my home
A place where I am not judged
A place I am supported and comforted
Family who loves me
Who I love in return
We share our ups and our downs
We get through the tough times
Together
A piece of my heart is in the digital world
With a family I call my own
And they are what keeps me
From falling apart in the real world.

Home

Home is where the heart is
And my heart lies in a digital world
A world where a family found me
Where they took me in
Loved me for me

They never ask me to change
But accept when i do
They comfort me and advise me
Not with empty words
But by sharing their experiences
And empathizing with me

We are separated by vast distances
And yet by none at all
The Internet has made it possible
For me in Iowa to connect
With a "sister" in Brazil
Age has no meaning to us
My "mother" is only 3 years older
My "daughter" less than a decade younger
But the love is very real

We connect outside of our digital world
One day when we meet
Our family will feel complete.

Thank You

I was so happy
When you found me again
Our reunion was not instant
Nor did our friendship rebuild fast
But slowly we talked more
Learned more about each other
Stuff we didn't know before
The miles between didn't matter
As we talked for hours
Sad we weren't close enough to see
I opened myself up
And shared things no one else knows
Things no one else would understand
You understood and accepted me
As I accepted you
Even during those times
When I'm not sure how to explain
You know what I mean
I was so relieved when we confessed

Our crushes on each other from so long ago
Glad to know it wasn't one-sided
Like I had always thought
When I mentioned moving closer
You got so excited
You still are and it keeps me motivated
I want to change my life

Make it better
Move closer
Have you in my life again
And you keep me focused on this dream
Thank you
For motivating me
For opening you heart
For accepting me
For finding me again
Thank you

Role Model

You are the strongest woman I know
You fight for your health
When you are only in your 30s
You have lost one eye
And are afraid for the other
You fight your heart
Get little sleep
You are fairly isolated
Alone much of the time

Yet, when those you love
Are sick or even sad
You worry about them
More than yourself
You put others before yourself
You push your eye to its limit
To the point you can barely see

You support and comfort
Your family and friends
Tell them not to worry about you
While you worry about them
You must feel lonely at times
But you rarely complain
You listen to rants
About silly troubles
And almost never rant yourself

You keep quiet
You tread softly
On others feelings
Even when they
Don't do the same
You love deeply
You are fiercely loyal
You are not afraid
To bare your scars
And fears
To those you love

You are more than a woman
You are a mother
Without giving birth
You are a sister
An aunt
Someone who can be counted on
You are outspoken
But kind
You are my role model

Extrospection

Dreams grow and change
As we ourselves do
As a child they seem
Limitless
We can do anything
Be anything
We have vast potential
As we grow
Our thoughts
And ambitions
Become more
Focused
We follow
Narrower paths
As we have more experiences
We change our minds
Shift directions
Like a sail
In the wind
Our boat
Changes course
People around us
Effect us
And can cause
Chain reactions
A love, a marriage,
A family

Setting aside a job
To be a parent
Setting aside old dreams
To realize new ones
Bad experiences
And relationships
Can cause us to withdraw
To be more cautious
Follow safer paths
While good relationships
And events
Can help heal our hearts
And get us moving
Forward
Help us to trust
And explore new paths
When the wind ceases
You have a choice
Do you sit and wait
Stagnant and still
Or do you pull out the oars
And chose to keep
Moving forward
To challenge yourself
To be strong
Even if you are
Frightened
Do you follow
The safe path
Or the adventure
That could await
Down the curving road
Do you move with the crowd

Or choose to make your own path
Be true to you
Remember as we live
Each experience
Each person
Effects us and helps us
Grow and change
Or holds us back
We choose
How to react
And which paths to follow
Do you move forward
Or stay in the past
Standing still
Or looking to the future
To new challenges
To new dreams
To new adventures
There will be hardships
There will be sadness and anger
But also happiness and love
The pain makes the good
All the sweeter

Where Am I?

Where am I?
I hear crickets chirp.
I hear owls hoot.
I hear the gentle wind,
Flowing through the tall grass.

Where am I?
I hear busy streets.
I hear noisy cars.
I hear the noises
One would hear in a crowded place.

Where am I?
I hear a bubbling brook.
I hear a fish jump.
I hear the quiet silence
Of the outdoors.

Where am I?
I'm in a meadow.
I'm in a city.
I'm in the woods
During a newborn spring.

Where am I?
Well wherever I am
I take you with me

Through the meadows, cities, and woods.
I never leave home
Without you in my heart and thoughts.

PART FOUR

A CONTRIBUTION

Too Close But Too Far

By Karter Anayah Blessing

On a computer somewhere
A pure and nice soul behind it
Waits for other souls there
Nice friends, fake guys
It's a whole new world to feel alive

But then you meet the right friends
They like the same things you do
You're not alone anymore,
bye sadness
Don't matter the distance,
they live in my heart
It makes me feel loved,
it makes me feel alive

I try to hit a teleport button
But it doesn't work
I patiently wait
My love isn't made by pixels
It's made by reality
I wait for the day something could happen
And the virtual reality could be alive

Made in the USA
San Bernardino, CA
17 February 2018